Ending South Sudan's Civil War

COUNCIL *on*
FOREIGN
RELATIONS

Center for Preventive Action

Council Special Report No. 77
November 2016

Kate Almquist Knopf

Ending South Sudan's Civil War

The Council on Foreign Relations (CFR) is an independent, nonpartisan membership organization, think tank, and publisher dedicated to being a resource for its members, government officials, business executives, journalists, educators and students, civic and religious leaders, and other interested citizens in order to help them better understand the world and the foreign policy choices facing the United States and other countries. Founded in 1921, CFR carries out its mission by maintaining a diverse membership, with special programs to promote interest and develop expertise in the next generation of foreign policy leaders; convening meetings at its headquarters in New York and in Washington, DC, and other cities where senior government officials, members of Congress, global leaders, and prominent thinkers come together with Council members to discuss and debate major international issues; supporting a Studies Program that fosters independent research, enabling CFR scholars to produce articles, reports, and books and hold roundtables that analyze foreign policy issues and make concrete policy recommendations; publishing *Foreign Affairs*, the preeminent journal on international affairs and U.S. foreign policy; sponsoring Independent Task Forces that produce reports with both findings and policy prescriptions on the most important foreign policy topics; and providing up-to-date information and analysis about world events and American foreign policy on its website, CFR.org.

The Council on Foreign Relations takes no institutional positions on policy issues and has no affiliation with the U.S. government. All views expressed in its publications and on its website are the sole responsibility of the author or authors.

Council Special Reports (CSRs) are concise policy briefs, produced to provide a rapid response to a developing crisis or contribute to the public's understanding of current policy dilemmas. CSRs are written by individual authors—who may be CFR fellows or acknowledged experts from outside the institution—in consultation with an advisory committee, and are intended to take sixty days from inception to publication. The committee serves as a sounding board and provides feedback on a draft report. It usually meets twice—once before a draft is written and once again when there is a draft for review; however, advisory committee members, unlike Task Force members, are not asked to sign off on the report or to otherwise endorse it. Once published, CSRs are posted on www.cfr.org.

For further information about CFR or this Special Report, please write to the Council on Foreign Relations, 58 East 68th Street, New York, NY 10065, or call the Communications office at 212.434.9888. Visit our website, CFR.org.

To submit a letter in response to a Council Special Report for publication on our website, CFR.org, you may send an email to CSReditor@cfr.org. Alternatively, letters may be mailed to us at: Publications Department, Council on Foreign Relations, 58 East 68th Street, New York, NY 10065. Letters should include the writer's name, postal address, and daytime phone number. Letters may be edited for length and clarity, and may be published online. Please do not send attachments. All letters become the property of the Council on Foreign Relations and will not be returned. We regret that, owing to the volume of correspondence, we cannot respond to every letter.

This report is printed on paper that is FSC ® Chain-of-Custody Certified by a printer who is certified by BM TRADA North America Inc.

Contents

Foreword

South Sudan, established in 2011, was like many countries before it born of civil war. What is both different and depressing, though, is that even after gaining independence and internationally recognized statehood, South Sudan, as a result of tribal and political conflict, is a country in name only. Civil war officially broke out in December 2013, sparked by political conflict between President Salva Kiir and then First Vice President Riek Machar. After years of fighting between their political factions and Dinka and Nuer tribes, Kiir and Machar agreed to reinstate a power-sharing agreement in August 2015. Less than a year later, in July 2016, the agreement collapsed, and with it any semblance of peace or political order. Both sides have been accused of war crimes, tribal conflict and militia violence is widespread, and the country is on the brink of economic collapse. Not surprisingly, the humanitarian situation is dire as tens of thousands have died and more than two million men, women, and children have been displaced.

In this Council Special Report, Kate Almquist Knopf, the director of the Africa Center for Strategic Studies at the National Defense University, describes how three years of civil war and the recently renewed violence have left South Sudan lacking in functioning institutions and depleted in resources. Past attempts to end the long-running conflict and stand the country up have failed despite extensive support—financial, political, and in the security sphere—from the African Union, the United Nations, and the United States.

All of this leads Almquist Knopf to the conclusion that the best option for South Sudan is a "clean break" from its leaders and power structures. Such a break would mean establishing an international transitional administration with the mandate of governing the country and building internal capacity that would allow self-rule. If this idea seems at all familiar, it might be because of its similarities to the trusteeships envisioned by the United Nations after World War II for entities making the transition from colony to independent country. What is striking is that, in this case, the notion of international trusteeship is being put forward for an already independent but failing country. It is the proverbial step back in the hopes that it will pave the way for steps forward. It is above all an exercise in realism.

Such a project could take ten to fifteen years or even longer. More specifically, the author envisions a peace intervention force of soldiers and police; a joint UN-African Union executive administration to provide basic services, oversee financial operations, and appoint ministers and personnel; and a negotiated exit for both Kiir and Machar, the major antagonists in South Sudan's recent history. Almquist Knopf's proposal acknowledges the need for involving neighboring states in any transitional arrangement, sustained U.S.-led diplomacy in the region and at the United Nations, and gaining the trust and support of the South Sudanese public, which is understandably fatigued from years of fighting and distrustful of both warring political factions. Importantly, she notes that the United States and others are already spending billions of dollars in aid and support for South Sudan; an international transitional administration would require continued investment on this scale, the difference being it promises better returns for the United States, the United Nations, and other donors.

The bold recommendations made in *Ending South Sudan's Civil War* are anything but guaranteed to work. There are many actors, internally and externally, who could undo such a policy. However, the status quo is clearly failing the country and its people, and Almquist Knopf's creative proposal deserves serious consideration. It could represent a way forward for South Sudan—and a model for what might well be needed elsewhere in Africa, the Middle East, and in other parts of the world when counties prove unable to govern themselves and provide for the security of either their citizens or their neighbors.

Richard N. Haass
President
Council on Foreign Relations
November 2016

Acknowledgments

This report has benefited immeasurably from the expertise of the members of the advisory committee and numerous others who contributed invaluable counsel on charting a new policy course to address such an extreme case of state collapse, particularly Chester A. Crocker, chair of the advisory committee and James R. Schlesinger Professor in the Practice of Strategic Studies at Georgetown University, and Princeton N. Lyman, former U.S. special envoy for Sudan and South Sudan. The U.S. Institute of Peace also provided vital assistance in researching previous cases of international executive mandates and authorities.

I am deeply grateful to the Council on Foreign Relations and the Center for Preventive Action for supporting this project at such a critical juncture for South Sudan and for the broader region. In particular, I am indebted to CPA's staff, including Director Paul B. Stares, Assistant Director Helia Ighani, and Research Associate Sarah Collman, for their insightful editing and resolute patience in guiding this report to publication as events on the ground shifted daily. Senior Vice President and Director of Studies James M. Lindsay and President Richard N. Haass helped to refine some of the more complex elements of the new policy approach recommended here. I am also grateful to CFR's Publications Department, including Editorial Director Patricia Lee Dorff, Production Editor Elizabeth Dana, Assistant Editor Sumit Poudyal, and Associate Editor Erik Crouch, who were instrumental in producing a high-caliber report in record time.

This publication was made possible by a grant from Carnegie Corporation of New York. The statements made and views expressed herein are solely my own.

Kate Almquist Knopf

Acronyms

AU	African Union
DRC	Democratic Republic of Congo
EU	European Union
FIB	Force Intervention Brigade
G10	Group of Ten
GEMAP	Governance and Economic Management Assistance Program
IGAD	Intergovernmental Authority on Development
IMF	International Monetary Fund
JMEC	Joint Monitoring and Evaluation Commission
L3	level 3
MONUSCO	United Nations Organization Stabilization Mission in the Democratic Republic of the Congo
M23	March 23
NTGL	National Transitional Government of Liberia
OHCHR	Office of the UN High Commissioner for Human Rights
PIC	Peace Implementation Council
PoC	protection of civilians
SNC	Supreme National Council
SPLA	Sudan People's Liberation Army
SPLM	Sudan People's Liberation Movement
SRSG	Special Representative of the Secretary-General
TGoNU	Transitional Government of National Unity
UNAMSIL	UN Assistance Mission in Sierra Leone

UNMIK	UN Interim Administration Mission in Kosovo
UNMISS	UN Mission in South Sudan
UNTAC	UN Transitional Authority in Cambodia
UNTAET	UN Transitional Administration in East Timor

Council Special Report

Introduction

After nearly three years of civil war, South Sudan has ceased to perform even the minimal functions and responsibilities of a sovereign state. It exercises no monopoly over coercive power, and its ability to deliver public services, provide basic security, and administer justice is virtually nonexistent. Although South Sudan may nominally enjoy juridical sovereignty, its domestic sovereignty is entirely contested and discredited, and nearly all of the warning signs of impending genocide are present: extreme tribal polarization fueling a cycle of revenge, widespread and systematic attacks against civilians, hate speech, atrocities intended to dehumanize particular populations, and targeting of community and tribal leaders, among others. The spillover effects of the worsening civil war will soon become intolerable for South Sudan's neighbors, who will likely conclude that the best option for sustaining their security and economic interests is to carve out spheres of influence in the country, leaving an unviable rump state in their wake.

The meltdown of the world's newest state poses a fundamental challenge to the international state system, to African and Western models of state-building, and to UN peacekeeping. Since 2005, the United States alone has devoted more than $11 billion in humanitarian, peacekeeping/security sector, and transition and reconstruction assistance to help the South Sudanese secure self-determination, with no end in sight.[1] UN peacekeeping in the two Sudans since 2004 has cost approximately $20 billion, the costliest peace interventions in the last decade, to which the United States has contributed more than a quarter of the funding.[2] While the U.S. government has sustained its commitment to humanitarian funding in South Sudan—allocating $1.9 billion in humanitarian assistance alone since the outbreak of the war in December 2013—U.S. taxpayers and the people of South Sudan deserve a better return on investment.

Given the extreme degree of South Sudan's state failure, the only remaining path to protect its sovereignty and territorial integrity, restore its legitimacy, and politically empower its citizens is through an international transitional administration, established by the United Nations and the African Union (AU), to run the country for a finite period.

Though seemingly radical, international administrations are not unprecedented and have been previously employed to guide Cambodia, Kosovo, East Timor, and other countries out of conflict. Because it will realistically take ten to fifteen years for the South Sudanese to develop a new vision for their state and the institutions to manage politics nonviolently, it is more sensible to plan for a long duration at the outset than to drift into an accumulation of one-year mandates over decades, as has happened in the eastern Democratic Republic of Congo (DRC), and elsewhere. Opposition to a UN and AU transitional administration could be mitigated through a combination of politics and force—by working with important South Sudanese constituencies frustrated with President Salva Kiir, former First Vice President Riek Machar, and their cronies; and then deploying a lean and agile peace intervention force to combat and deter the remaining spoilers once they have been politically isolated.

Brokering such a transition will require committed diplomacy by the United States in close partnership with African governments. This transition would not, however, necessitate an investment costlier than the current approach and, in fact, promises a better chance of success. Like a patient in critical condition, South Sudan can be restored to viability only by putting it on life support and then gradually withdrawing assistance.

Challenges to Peace and Security in South Sudan

On July 9, 2011, the longest civil war in Africa ended when South Sudan gained independence from Sudan, after an internationally recognized referendum on self-determination. On December 15, 2013, South Sudan descended into its own civil war, when a simmering political struggle among President Kiir, First Vice President Machar, and other elites over the leadership of the country's governing party, the Sudan People's Liberation Movement (SPLM), sparked fighting in the capital, Juba. Amid specious allegations that Machar and a group of ministers whom Kiir had dismissed several months earlier had attempted a coup, Machar fled Juba, and the fighting quickly devolved into a tribal and factional conflict throughout the country.

The African Union, the United Nations, the United States, and other Western powers subsequently expended significant diplomatic efforts to negotiate an end to the fighting. In August 2015, largely as a result of the threat of targeted UN sanctions against senior individuals on both sides of the conflict and of the imposition of a UN arms embargo, Machar, then Kiir, signed a power-sharing agreement (see text box on the structure of the agreement), which had been mediated by the Intergovernmental Authority on Development (IGAD), the regional organization promoting trade, cooperation, and development that includes South Sudan and seven other East African nations.

The agreement facilitated Machar's return to Juba in April 2016 and the subsequent formation of the Transitional Government of National Unity (TGoNU). In July 2016, however, fighting again broke out between Kiir's and Machar's forces in Juba. Machar fled the city for the second time, leading to the de facto collapse of the transitional government, escalating violence that could spiral into genocide, and a worsening of the threat to regional security. After Machar's flight from the capital, military forces loyal to Kiir—the Sudan People's Liberation Army (SPLA)—undertook an effort to kill him and his forces, the SPLM-in Opposition, through a coordinated operation

involving ground troops and a bombing campaign in Western Equatoria State. Even before Juba descended into violence in July 2016, the
two main parties to the agreement and other armed actors had been
violating the permanent cease-fire on a daily basis, and decision-
making within the TGoNU had been paralyzed.[3]

The failure of the agreement and the de facto collapse of the TGoNU
was as predictable as it was inevitable. Negotiated settlements that have

STRUCTURE OF THE AGREEMENT
ON THE RESOLUTION OF CONFLICT
IN SOUTH SUDAN

The August 2015 agreement provided for a power-sharing Transitional Government of National Unity (TGoNU) for thirty months
to oversee an ambitious plan for political, security, and economic
reforms, including the approval of a permanent constitution and
elections for a new government.

The agreement was signed by Kiir on behalf of the Sudan People's Liberation Movement-in Government, Machar on behalf of
the Sudan People's Liberation Movement-in Opposition, former
Sudan People's Liberation Movement (SPLM) Secretary General Pagan Amun on behalf of a group of former senior ministers
and SPLM leaders who broke with Kiir and were arrested in the
course of the events of December 2013 (known as the Group of
Ten [G10] or "former detainees"), and Lam Akol on behalf of
South Sudan's "other political parties." Power in the executive
and legislative branches as well as at the state level was allocated to
the government and the opposition in a 53-33 split. The remaining
14 percent was divided evenly among the G10 and other political
parties. The functioning of the executive was premised on "colle-
gial decision-making" among three figures representing the three
major tribal groups in the country: the president (Kiir, a Dinka),
the first vice president (Machar, a Nuer, whom Kiir replaced in
late July 2016 with another Nuer, Taban Deng Gai), and the vice
president (James Wani Igga, an Equatorian). Deadlocks within
the executive were to be broken by a two-thirds vote of the council of ministers. The president was the commander in chief of the

ended other civil wars have normally required at least three conditions for success. First, the parties need to believe that a military solution is impossible. Second, the negotiated agreement needs to offer an equitable and sustainable distribution of power that includes—but is not limited to—the "compromised elites," as well as protections for minorities. Third, the parties need to believe that the terms of the agreement will be enforced over time.[4] None of these conditions are present in South Sudan.

armed forces. Machar was to remain commander of the opposition forces until their integration into the national military.

In addition to envisioning over twenty commissions, committees, and authorities—on issues ranging from anticorruption to refugees, truth and reconciliation, and roads—the agreement also established a Ceasefire and Transitional Security Arrangements Monitoring Mechanism comprising twenty-one members from the warring parties, South Sudanese civil society, and the witnesses and guarantors of the agreement. A Strategic Defense and Review Board—composed of South Sudanese representing the warring parties, the national assembly, and civil society—was to lead the security sector transformation.

The agreement stipulated the establishment of a Joint Monitoring and Evaluation Commission (JMEC) to monitor and oversee its implementation, the TGoNU, and various transitional structures. In October 2015, former Botswanan President Festus Mogae was appointed by the Intergovernmental Authority on Development (IGAD) to chair the thirty-two-member JMEC, composed of representatives of the parties, other South Sudanese actors, and the international guarantors and witnesses to the agreement. The JMEC operates on consensus or, if needed, by a simple majority vote. The JMEC was charged with reporting non-implementation of the agreement and other "deficiencies" to the TGoNU and recommending "corrective action." The JMEC could also report at any time—and make recommendations for remedial action—to the IGAD chairman, the chair of the AU Commission, the AU Peace and Security Council, the UN Secretary-General, and the UN Security Council.

Instead, tribal and political violence continue because the parties to the conflict have not credibly forsaken a military solution, the four cease-fires to which they have agreed since January 2014 have been consistently violated, and various tribal communities increasingly view military action as their only recourse to what they perceive as an existential threat posed by either Kiir's or Machar's factions. The August 2015 agreement attempted to restore a power-sharing arrangement that had already failed once before and was predicated on two individuals who are irredeemably compromised among competing tribal communities. Moreover, the near-total deficit of legitimate power and institutions in South Sudan means there is little power to actually share. Finally, the monitoring mechanisms established under the agreement and the current UN peacekeeping mission have minimal enforcement abilities.

CONTINUATION OF TRIBAL AND POLITICAL VIOLENCE

Each of the political and military factors that the United Nations uses to determine the risk of genocide is present in South Sudan, and the possibility of even larger mass atrocities is strong.[5] The continued armed conflict is largely rooted in a perception among core partisans on all sides that they are fighting an existential struggle against domination by either Kiir or Machar. Both Dinka and Nuer leaders—members of Kiir's and Machar's tribes, respectively—have increasingly used inflammatory, polarizing, and ethnically demeaning rhetoric against one another and against other tribal groups, even though the descent into war was initially triggered by a political, rather than a tribal, dispute.

Many Nuer claim that Kiir personally ordered the massacres in Juba following the alleged coup in December 2013. The AU Commission of Inquiry on South Sudan led by former Nigerian President Olusegun Obasanjo supported this assertion, concluding that the killings in Juba in December 2013 constituted war crimes and crimes against humanity and "were committed pursuant to or in furtherance of a State policy."[6] Nuer are therefore fighting not on behalf of Machar but to protect their community and, in some cases, for revenge.[7]

The Dinka—who constitute a majority of the government leadership and the military and security services, as well as a plurality of the population—similarly believe that Machar and his forces harbor an anti-Dinka agenda. The AU Commission of Inquiry also found forces under Machar's command responsible for war crimes and crimes against humanity.[8] Senior Dinka leaders and government officials, including Kiir, regularly cite the 1991 massacre in Bor, Jonglei State, as evidence of the Nuer's ingrained hatred for the Dinka. As the leader of a breakaway faction of the SPLM during the Sudanese Civil War in the 1990s, Machar commanded forces that attacked and massacred approximately five thousand Dinka, mainly civilians, in Bor, the hometown of then SPLM leader John Garang, also a Dinka.

Even before the renewed violence in Juba in July 2016, reasons to fear more deadly episodes of ethnic violence abounded.[9] The site in Juba where the mostly Nuer opposition troops deployed to accompany Machar upon his return in April 2016 was near both an SPLA installation and a UN protection of civilians (PoC) site housing more than twenty-eight thousand displaced Nuer. The government alleges that the PoC site is a bastion of opposition fighters, despite the fact that the majority of its residents are women and children.

Similarly, only a handful of SPLA soldiers had deployed to cantonment sites twenty-five kilometers outside Juba, and the capital itself was far from demilitarized, contrary to the government's obligations under the agreement. In addition to the thousands of SPLA soldiers still in Juba, credible reports indicated that several thousand plainclothes National Security Service personnel began to deploy to the capital as early as January 2016. These contingents were heavily armed, predominantly Dinka, and under the direct command of individuals whom the AU Commission of Inquiry on South Sudan, the UN Panel of Experts, and other independent bodies have identified as primarily responsible for some of the worst violence to date.[10]

Moreover, an executive order issued by Kiir in October 2015 to increase the number of states in South Sudan from ten to twenty-eight—a move that contradicted some of the core provisions of the peace agreement and is perceived to advantage Kiir's Dinka tribe—has aggravated tribal tensions and added another driver to the conflict. Although welcomed by some South Sudanese communities, Kiir's order neglected to specify a process for demarcating contentious state borders and so has further stoked grievances among already restive minority tribes. The implementation of the order has proceeded even after the transitional government was formed in April 2016, despite the demands of IGAD and the chair of the Joint Monitoring and Evaluation Commission (JMEC), former Botswanan President Festus Mogae, to suspend it.[11] (The JMEC monitors and oversees the implementation of the August 2015 power-sharing agreement, the transitional government, and various transitional structures [see text box].) Kiir's executive order has also encouraged the government and affiliated militia to force displacements of particular communities from certain localities; this could be the beginning of organized ethnic cleansing. The February 2016 attack on the UN PoC site in Malakal, during which the SPLA facilitated the safe transport of Dinka civilians from the site before reentering the camp with allied militias and destroying the Nuer and Shilluk areas, was a stark indicator of the war's trajectory.[12]

Tribal polarization has resulted in a conflict that is no longer binary—whether Kiir versus Machar or the Dinka versus the Nuer—and increasingly factious armed actors are jockeying for political and military advantage to defend their communities and shape the landscape following Machar's departure from Juba in July 2016. For example, Shilluk commander Johnson Olony, who defected from the SPLA to the opposition in the spring of 2015, heads one of the most potent fighting forces in Upper Nile State but remains only nominally aligned with Machar. Prior to 2016, the Equatorians—one of the three main tribal groups in South Sudan, along with the Dinka and the Nuer—had mostly remained on the sidelines of the war but have since become involved in full-scale hostilities against the government and Dinka civilians, including attacks on the outskirts of Juba. These attacks have precipitated reprisals by the SPLA and Dinka militias as well as an escalation of inflammatory rhetoric between Dinka and Equatorians. Machar has attempted to sway the Equatorian armed groups to ally with him militarily, an effort that has gained momentum since he fled from Juba, which is in the greater Equatoria region.

REPEAT OF A FAILED POLITICAL SETTLEMENT

The August 2015 agreement attempted to restore the same political bargain that had collapsed in December 2013—a power-sharing arrangement between Kiir and Machar. The agreement neglected to address the long-standing struggle between the two leaders and their constituencies for political and economic power as well as the added grievances from nearly three years of civil war. Therefore, continuing to use the agreement as a basis for conflict resolution will only escalate human suffering and regional instability. As former U.S. Assistant Secretary of State for African Affairs Chester A. Crocker notes, historically "if outside states attempt to freeze power relations or entrench political-military groups in open-ended power-sharing structures, they will likely sow seeds of future conflict and distort the chances for organic political development ([e.g.,] Lebanon and Bosnia)."[13] The tacit U.S. endorsement of Kiir's decision in July 2016 to appoint the opposition's former chief negotiator, Taban Deng Gai, to replace Machar—both Deng Gai and Machar are Nuer—as first vice president is a case in point. Deng Gai has no meaningful political constituency and is reviled across the country, including by important communities within his own tribe, for being extraordinarily corrupt and self-promoting. Rather than shoring up the viability of the agreement, Deng Gai's appointment further incited opponents of Kiir and the government to pursue violence as their only recourse.

State sovereignty is not innate but contingent and dynamic, based on a constant and evolving interplay between public and private authorities that determines a state's strength or weakness.[14] The current power-sharing arrangement perpetuates a dynamic among the nascent public authorities the state and its ruling elite—and the prevailing private authorities, such as the Jieng Council of Elders, a self-appointed group of Dinka politicians from the Bahr el Ghazal region who have exerted significant influence on Kiir, and various nonstate armed groups.[15] This dynamic has obliterated the capacity of the state to deliver safety or services to its people, preventing consolidation of the state over the long term.[16] The challenge for the United States and South Sudan's neighbors is to construct a credible pathway for the endogenous development of public authority embodied in a new social compact—in other words, to enable the conditions that foster South Sudan's legitimacy and practical sovereignty.

Kiir's twenty-eight-states decree—the most flagrant but by no means the only instance of a direct contravention of the constitution and the August 2015 agreement—undermined the power-sharing formula at the center of the agreement and injected new local drivers into the conflict. Even before the de facto collapse of the TGoNU, Kiir and Machar had taken few tangible steps to reverse the political elite's predatory and destructive behavior toward the population—including war crimes such as the systematic targeting of civilians—or even to maintain a cease-fire.

Mogae, in a statement to the JMEC on June 23, 2016, declared, "The progress I had expected has not materialized. If anything, the Parties are further apart. There appears to be a stalemate that now threatens the implementation of the entire Agreement." And later in his statement, he noted the "lack of commitment towards peace" and the "meager gains we are all making in the peace process."[17] On July 31, 2016, after Machar had fled Juba, Mogae reported to the JMEC partners during a meeting in Khartoum: "We know that forces of both parties and others allied to them continue to clash throughout the country, with a likelihood of larger battles increasing every day."[18] As he said on June 23, "This deliberate and institutionalized impediment to the implementation of the Agreement is totally unacceptable."[19]

South Sudan's increasing tribal polarization further complicates the prospects for a viable power-sharing arrangement that could repair the rifts in the country, particularly absent a meaningful mechanism for guaranteeing minority rights. The trend toward more illegitimate and unorganized devolution and decentralization—whether by government decree or by minorities asserting autonomy in self-defense—adds to the chaos and potential for further predation and local state capture.

LACK OF POLITICAL LEGITIMACY

Conflict persists in South Sudan not because of an imbalance of power but because of the near total deficit of legitimate power. The elite competition that sparked the civil war is symptomatic, rather than causal, of this power vacuum. Because South Sudan has no history of meaningful governance—during the colonial period, prior to its secession from Sudan, or since independence—its politics lack not just the institutions for the distribution of power but sufficient legitimate power to distribute. This power deficit magnifies the challenges posed by the state's lack of capacity.

As the AU Commission of Inquiry determined, "the crisis in South Sudan is primarily attributable to the inability of relevant institutions to mediate and manage conflicts, which spilt out into the army, and subsequently the general population." The commission further found that previous state-building initiatives in South Sudan, which had focused on capacity-building, appear to "have failed," a conclusion, it notes, not arrived at solely by foreigners but in keeping with the results of a comprehensive review commissioned by Kiir's office before the outbreak of the war. The commission attributed this failure to a number of factors but noted that international state-building initiatives tended to concentrate on technical interventions and ignored politics.[20]

The current national government is a loose network of individuals with varying and competing degrees of coercive force at their disposal but no political center of gravity. Kiir's legitimacy has eroded significantly since the outbreak of the war, due not only to his own misdeeds but also the chipping away of his authority by ambitious competitors within the regime. South Sudanese politics lack an individual of significant stature or credibility to take Kiir's place and unite the country's disparate factions. The SPLM, which led the country's decades-long independence struggle, has effectively imploded. Therefore, ending the war will require not merely balancing or dispersing power within the system but creating a framework to inject power, authority, and legitimacy into South Sudanese politics.[21]

INADEQUACY OF ENFORCEMENT MECHANISMS

The UN Mission in South Sudan (UNMISS) is not prepared to intervene to avert confrontation between government and opposition forces or to enforce the August 2015 agreement. This inadequacy was evident in early July 2016, when UNMISS halted all patrols while Juba descended into mass violence.[22] Kiir's government has consistently challenged UNMISS and JMEC, including through military attacks on UNMISS personnel and the expulsion of UNMISS and JMEC staff from South Sudan. However, the agreement's guarantors, including the IGAD member states and the United States, have imposed no tangible punishment, fostering the parties' disregard for these mechanisms.

Following a request by the IGAD heads of state in July 2016, the UN Security Council adopted a resolution to establish a regional protection force within UNMISS to "create an enabling environment for implementation of the Agreement."[23] Despite intermittent rhetorical acceptance of the force, the government has consistently obstructed any progress toward its deployment. Even if the government ultimately acquiesces, the protection force has a limited mandate: to ensure movement in and out of Juba, protect the airport, and prevent attacks on UN and humanitarian personnel—not to enforce provisions of the agreement, which has in any case effectively collapsed.

Costs and Consequences of the War

Nearly three years after the civil war began, armed conflict and mass violence against civilians continue unabated, South Sudan's economy is in shambles, and a humanitarian catastrophe threatens three-quarters of the population. If left to its present course, the demise of South Sudan will compound the threats already posed by state failure, weak governance, regional conflicts, migration, and extremism to the other states in the Horn of Africa, a region set to more than double in population between 2015 and 2050.

UNCHECKED VIOLENCE

Even before the eruption of fighting in Juba in July, South Sudanese civilians were enduring relentless, widespread atrocities in a recurring pattern of violence that took root in the early days of the war and that the AU Commission of Inquiry characterized as amounting to war crimes and crimes against humanity.[24] Violence against civilians now extends to most regions of the country, including those not directly implicated in the primary political or tribal cleavages that sparked the conflict.

While there is no recent estimate of the total number of conflict-related casualties since fighting began in December 2013—the only commonly cited figure being fifty thousand deaths as of November 2014—humanitarian officials privately believe that, given that the war in South Sudan disproportionately affects civilians, total civilian deaths in South Sudan may already exceed those in Syria, out of a population roughly half that of Syria's, in half as much time.[25] Conservative estimates have placed mortality rates in some areas at two to three times the internationally accepted emergency threshold of one death per ten thousand people per day.[26] An estimated 7,165 civilians were killed in just five counties of one state in South Sudan over a twelve-month period in 2014–2015—more than twice the number of civilians killed across Yemen in a year of war there.[27]

ECONOMIC COLLAPSE

South Sudan's economic situation is dire. The International Monetary Fund (IMF) warned in June 2016 of "a risk of total economic collapse" and a macroeconomic situation in which "imbalances are large and economic buffers are exhausted."[28] Foreign exchange receipts and government revenues, over 98 percent of which come from oil sales, have plummeted as world oil prices have collapsed and the war has disrupted oil production.

At the same time as government revenues have plummeted, liberalization of the exchange rate in December 2015 has resulted in a nearly 90 percent devaluation of the South Sudanese pound. Inflation reached close to 700 percent in September 2016 and continues to mount, and the government could face more than $1.1 billion—25 percent of the gross domestic product—in deficits in the 2016–2017 fiscal year.[29] Moreover, prices of basic commodities have skyrocketed as real wages have plunged, exacerbating the country's already severe food crisis, especially among market-dependent households in urban areas. For instance, the price of sorghum in Juba in March 2016 was 400 percent above the five-year average.[30]

HUMANITARIAN CATASTROPHE

In 2014 and 2015, the United Nations designated South Sudan a level 3 (L3) humanitarian emergency, a designation reserved for the most severe complex humanitarian emergencies; South Sudan was one of only four such emergencies in the world and the only one in Africa.[31] Thus far in 2016, the humanitarian crisis has worsened. In mid-September, South Sudan joined Syria, Afghanistan, and Somalia as one of only four countries with more than one million refugees outside its borders.[32] More than 1.6 million people have been displaced internally, including nearly 200,000 seeking refuge at UN PoC sites or in front of UN bases; 4.8 million (approximately 40 percent of the population) face severe food shortages; and more than 8 million (approximately 75 percent) face some degree of food insecurity, the highest level of hunger since the war began.[33]

THREAT TO REGIONAL STABILITY

South Sudan's dissolution poses an increasingly significant threat to the stability of the Horn of Africa and to the security of strategic U.S. partners in the region, particularly given these partner states' propensity to undertake unilateral military interventions, with unpredictable consequences.[34] The United States has substantial political, financial, and military investments in the states most affected by South Sudan's war, such as Ethiopia, Uganda, and Kenya. These and other states are already wrestling with crises of their own: the ongoing conflict in Somalia, the escalating war in Yemen, increased volatility in Kenya preceding the 2017 presidential elections, the internal conflicts in Sudan, and deadly political protests as well as devastating drought in Ethiopia.

Intraregional tensions—such as the long-standing rivalry between Sudan and Uganda and the competition for regional hegemony between Uganda and Ethiopia—abound, and both worsen and are worsened by South Sudan's conflict. The war has also stimulated simmering ethnic rivalries in the states where the South Sudanese have sought refuge. Communal fighting broke out on Ethiopia's side of the border with South Sudan in early 2016, for instance, and Ethiopian troops were deployed into South Sudan's Jonglei State in April 2016 following a particularly brazen incursion into Ethiopia's Gambella region by a South Sudanese tribal militia.[35]

Recommendations:
A Clean Break for South Sudan

States successfully emerging from conflict have managed the transition in one of three ways—by relying on existing authorities to manage the process, by creating a new power-sharing arrangement, or by engineering a clean break from the past that essentially establishes a new governing authority, usually with major international support.[36]

In South Sudan, the first model would involve less international involvement and oversight than was envisioned in the August 2015 agreement and would therefore not be a credible alternative to the current failed approach. The August 2015 agreement, which has collapsed, reflects the second model. The third model, in which South Sudan can temporarily draw power and legitimacy from other sources during an international transitional administration, therefore remains the only viable option.

The most extreme cases of state failure have demanded more than third-party security guarantees or support for capacity-building. When, as political scientists David Lake and Christopher Fariss have shown, the state exercises only "limited or abused sovereignty," international trusteeship—used sparingly—can break a vicious circle in which narrow, extractive coalitions and competition for state control have led to a "vortex that pulls states down."[37] In these instances, the objective is not capacity-building but limiting violence and shepherding a transition to a new, more legitimate governing order by leveling the playing field among belligerents. The effectiveness of trusteeship is, however, contingent on two factors: first, the trustee has few, if any, interests beyond stability in the failed state; second, the interests of the trustee and the average citizen overlap.[38] While an international transitional administration should come at the request of the South Sudanese, these conditions for success would nonetheless exist in South Sudan should the United Nations and the AU lead the transitional administration.

Precedents exist for external administration in other countries transitioning from civil wars.[39] The degree of corruption and the dearth of capacity at all levels of government in South Sudan is as severe as it was in Liberia, for example, when donor governments insisted on dual-key controls over the state's finances and on rebuilding the Liberian Armed Forces from the ground up during the country's transition from civil war.[40] Even the rudimentary institutions that South Sudan had in place at independence could not possibly recover without public administration support from external actors. Lack of capacity aside, since 2005, the country's leaders have squandered tens of billions of dollars from oil revenue, bankrupting the state, and there is no evidence to suggest they would improve their financial management practices in the future.

Potential opposition to an international transitional administration could be overcome if a UN and AU executive mandate were implemented through a well-choreographed, U.S.-led diplomatic process that accounted for the unique political dynamics in South Sudan and the interests of its neighbors and other African states.

Application of the clean break model in the South Sudanese context would need to account for the lack of legitimate power within the country, afford an opportunity to address the power struggle between the two leaders and the added grievances of the civil war, and provide a new framework for empowering the South Sudanese to take ownership of their future and broker a new compact between state and society, including through appropriate transitional justice and reconciliation mechanisms.[41]

Specifically, the international transitional administration should accomplish the following objectives, consistent with previous international executive mandates (see appendix):

- *Maintain territorial integrity and restore order and public security.* The transitional administration should provide basic security to preclude foreign intervention and occupation, to defuse the need for local self-defense forces, to neutralize militias, to disarm civilians, and to allow time to delink the military from politics—including the ruling party—and the economy by building professional security services that meet citizen needs.[42]

- *Provide basic governance and administration of essential public services.* The transitional administration should ensure delivery of basic public services (e.g., health, education, clean water and sanitation, etc.), stabilize the humanitarian situation, and facilitate the return of internally displaced persons and refugees to their homes as well as the recovery of their livelihoods as soon as conditions permit voluntary return.

- *Rebuild the economy.* The transitional administration should undertake an economic bailout package to restore macroeconomic stability in the short term and to provide some construction of critical infrastructure to connect the country and support economic recovery.

- *Establish the political and constitutional framework for the transition to full sovereignty.* The transitional administration should defer elections until reconciliation, accountability, and national dialogue processes culminate in a new permanent constitution, thereby removing the prospect of winner-takes-all elections looming over political, security, and institutional reforms.

Critically, an international transitional administration should provide space for the kind of "national process" prescribed by the AU Commission of Inquiry "to provide a forum for dialogue, inquiry and to record the multiple, often competing narratives about South Sudan's history and conflicts; to construct a common narrative around which a new South Sudan can orient its future; to uncover and document the history of victimization and to recommend appropriate responses," including through a truth and reconciliation commission.

As the AU Commission of Inquiry determined, "the demands for federalism in sections of society are essentially about popular participation, service delivery, and guarantees for autonomy for South Sudanese in different parts of the country to decide on local priorities based on the principle of subsidiarity."[43] Therefore, political access for all citizens is crucial in moving past the civil war and a history of weak governance and exclusion. A national process, initiated by the transitional administration, would facilitate an endogenous discussion on state structure and lay the groundwork for a more integrated society.

Finally, the mandate duration of the international transitional administration (ten to fifteen years, which is realistic given the nature of the tasks to be accomplished) would be crucial to end violent jockeying for electoral advantage and to refocus politics on building the legitimacy of public authorities and basic trust in them, then allowing public institutions to emerge as the international support is gradually withdrawn.

COMPONENTS OF AN INTERNATIONAL TRANSITIONAL ADMINISTRATION

UN and AU Executive Mandate: At the request of South Sudan and with the support of the regional states, full executive authority would be vested in an international administration for ten to fifteen years. The transitional administrator would have the power to appoint and remove ministers, state governors, and other officials as well as to veto laws and legislation counter to inclusive, equitable, rules-based governance. Executive, managerial, and working-level personnel in government ministries, authorities, committees, and agencies would be vetted for professional qualifications and could be replaced with non–South Sudanese while a new civil service is developed; qualified South Sudanese technocrats would be retained.

The international administration would have the final say on budget receipts, expenditures, and procurements. Oil sales—South Sudan's primary source of revenue—would be managed by the World Bank through an international escrow account and would prioritize funding service delivery and economic recovery in consultation with the transitional administration. In contrast to the practices of Kiir's government, the allocation of oil revenue would be publicly transparent to the South Sudanese.

Advisory Council: Composed of representatives from the SPLM-in Government (excluding Kiir), the SPLM-in Opposition (excluding Machar), other political parties, tribal elders, and civil society, an advisory council would be established to advise the transitional UN and AU administration. Membership in this council, however, would require a commitment to the structure and timeline of the transition.

Peace Intervention Force: A critical component of an international transitional administration would be a credible peace intervention force to restore basic security. The force, while requiring robust rules of engagement, an effective command structure, and assets to enable mobility, would need not exceed the size or cost of the current UNMISS force. In a political context where core elements of government and opposition forces would not oppose and would likely welcome the international transitional administration as the least bad alternative in the wake of the August 2015 agreement's failure, a primarily African force comprising four to five battalions (approximately 4,250 soldiers) and 3,500 police—significantly fewer troops than are currently deployed under UNMISS—with a demonstrated willingness to use deadly force could be deployed. In fact, security arrangements that have successfully ended other civil wars prioritized the demonstration of a convincing commitment to enforcement rather than massive deployment or a widespread use of force.

Separate from the civilian administration but under the command authority of the transitional administrator, the peace intervention force would not be a countrywide military deployment but an agile, battalion-sized presence in the four or five main areas of conflict, including the capital, and the main population centers: Unity State, Upper Nile State, Jonglei State, Western and Central Equatoria states, possibly Western Bahr el Ghazal State, and Juba. Each battalion of eight hundred fifty troops could comprise three quick reaction force units, with the air assets to deploy rapidly within their area of operation and confront emerging threats. An additional support battalion as well as five formed police units of seven hundred personnel each could also be deployed.

Similarly structured peacekeeping missions have been deployed in Liberia and Ivory Coast, parallel to existing civilian governance structures; the larger of the two, the UN Operation in Côte d'Ivoire had an annual budget of approximately $400 million at its height and never exceeded seven thousand troops. By contrast, the current annual budget for UNMISS, which comprises thirteen thousand troops and two thousand police personnel in addition to a substantial civilian component, is $1.1 billion, 28 percent of which the United States pays. UNMISS's ability to protect civilians outside the seven UN PoC sites, however, has been limited. In February 2016, UNMISS was unable (or unwilling) to even prevent or stop the attack on the PoC site in Malakal.[44]

The Force Intervention Brigade (FIB) within the United Nations Organization Stabilization Mission in the Democratic Republic of the Congo (MONUSCO) also provides an instructive case. With its four thousand troops (within the broader MONUSCO force of nineteen thousand), the FIB was able to neutralize the security threat posed by the March 23 (M23) rebel movement in 2013 and 2014, not because it substantially improved MONUSCO's overall operational effectiveness but for two other reasons. First, the troop-contributing countries—South Africa, Tanzania, and Malawi—demonstrated a clear willingness to exercise their Chapter VII mandate under the UN Charter in engaging the M23 in direct combat. Second, the composition of the force exemplified a credible political commitment by African states to confront the M23 and its principal regional backer, Rwanda. Faced with a demonstrable commitment of political and military will, the M23 effectively dissolved.

The FIB was not, however, the first UN force to effectively engage in combat with spoilers to an internationally endorsed peace effort. In 1999, the UN Assistance Mission in Sierra Leone (UNAMSIL) confronted the Revolutionary United Front; in 2007, the UN Interim Force in Lebanon was mandated to "extend the authority of the state" by disbanding illegal armed groups; and the same year, the UN Stabilization Mission in Haiti battled gangs in Cité Soleil.[45]

Although eastern DRC, Liberia, Ivory Coast, Sierra Leone, Lebanon, and Haiti are much smaller geographically than South Sudan, the lessons of credible political and military force apply. A peace intervention force for South Sudan would focus on directly combating politically isolated spoilers, such as Kiir's inner circle and close family members, in the principal theaters of conflict and population centers through a credible military deterrent rather than large-scale, countrywide combat operations. As such an approach would be predicated on gaining support of states in the region by accommodating their interests, none of the protagonists under this scenario would enjoy the same state backing that the M23 received from Rwanda.

Given its leading role in bringing about South Sudan's independence, the United States could also consider an over-the-horizon force consisting of one battalion based in the region to provide in extremis assurances to the peace intervention force and further reinforce its deterrent effect. In 2000, the United Kingdom positioned a brigade of ships off the coast of Sierra Leone in support of UNAMSIL, and in 2006, the European Union (EU) deployed a standby force of 1,200 to Gabon as part of the international peacekeeping support for elections in DRC. Although the United States has not previously made such a commitment in Africa, the U.S. military has pre-positioned personnel in Uganda to possibly evacuate U.S. citizens from South Sudan. In addition, the United States maintains a permanent military base in Djibouti.

ROAD MAP TOWARD THE INTERNATIONAL TRANSITIONAL ADMINISTRATION

The United States should work with regional and international partners to pursue the following course of action leading to the formation of an international transitional administration.

A Negotiated Exit for Kiir and Machar

For an international transitional administration to succeed, Kiir would need to willingly relinquish power and he and Machar would need to be peacefully excluded from meaningful participation in South Sudan's political life and governance; this requires that they be sufficiently deterred from opposing the transitional administration. As the AU Commission of Inquiry noted in October 2014, based on broad consultations with South Sudanese:

> A majority of respondents on both sides of the conflict were of the view that both principals in the crisis, President Salva Kiir and [First Vice President] Riek Machar, were to be held responsible for the crisis, its escalation and the violations perpetrated. While there is a lack of clarity from views expressed on the form that responsibility should take, the Commission's conception includes criminal, civil or political (administrative) elements.[46]

Given that Kiir and Machar are both widely discredited, their permanent exit from South Sudanese politics would give an immediate boost of credibility and support to a transitional UN and AU administration.

The reports of the AU Commission of Inquiry, the Office of the UN High Commissioner for Human Rights (OHCHR), and other bodies provide a credible basis for the indictment and trial of both Kiir and Machar (as well as many others) for war crimes and crimes against humanity by the International Criminal Court or the Hybrid Court for South Sudan envisioned in the August 2015 agreement. To expedite their departure from the political scene, the United States—with the support of South Sudan's neighbors—could offer Kiir and Machar immunity from international prosecution and safe haven abroad in exchange for Kiir's willingness to hand over power to a UN and AU administration and a commitment from both Kiir and Machar never to hold or contest power again and to remain permanently outside South Sudan.

To give the threat of prosecution credibility, underscore the determination to pursue an international transitional administration, and strongly deter Kiir and Machar from remaining involved in South Sudanese politics, the United States should press the AU to establish the Hybrid Court for South Sudan immediately, lead the UN Security Council to institute time-triggered sanctions on both individuals as well as an arms embargo on South Sudan, and work with the United

Kingdom and other like-minded states to put preemptive contract sanctions in place.

- *Hybrid Court.* The August 2015 agreement requires that the transitional government enact legislation to establish a court to investigate and prosecute individuals responsible for violations of international and South Sudanese law from December 15, 2013, through the end of the transitional period. According to the agreement, the majority of all judges, as well as the prosecutors and defense counsel, are to come from African states other than South Sudan. The AU chair is mandated to appoint the judges, prosecutors, and defense counsel. The United States is well placed to press the AU at the highest levels to proceed with these appointments as well as to encourage respected African leaders, such as former Nigerian President Olusegun Obasanjo, who led the AU Commission of Inquiry, to publicly support JMEC chair Mogae's request—in his first report to the AU Peace and Security Council in January 2016—for the prosecutor to begin preparing cases.[47] Although the prosecutor would ultimately determine whom to try, the tangible prospect of trial for Kiir, Machar, and other high-level perpetrators is necessary to ensure the departure of the two leaders and to induce cooperation of other senior officials who might fear prosecution.

- *Time-triggered sanction designations.* In March 2015, the UN Security Council established a sanctions regime on South Sudan allowing for the imposition of travel bans and asset freezes on individuals deemed to be obstructing the peace process, breaching cease-fire agreements, and violating international humanitarian and human rights law, among other criteria. In its final report on January 22, 2016, the independent UN Panel of Experts established to advise the Security Council on sanctions provided clear and convincing evidence that Kiir, Machar, and other senior officials in the government bore responsibility for the full range of actions that the Security Council determined were grounds for sanctions. This evidence has been corroborated by reports from the OHCHR, the AU Commission of Inquiry, and others. The United States should introduce a Security Council resolution to impose sanctions on Kiir, Machar, and other senior figures from both warring parties if they do not relinquish power and depart the country by a specified date. Russia and China would be unlikely to veto such a resolution provided South Sudan's neighbors support the overall approach toward an international transitional administration.

- *Preemptive contract sanctions.* The United States and other partners could declare that the successor governments of South Sudan would not be legally bound by contracts that the existing regime signs. This declaration would cast a shadow on current oil and natural resource concessions and deter the signing of new contracts, effectively closing off the promise of additional proceeds from mortgaging the country's resources. Given that the United States and the United Kingdom host the majority of sovereign debt contracts, an announcement from these two states alone would have a significant effect on investment because claims would be nearly impossible to enforce.[48]

- *Comprehensive arms embargo.* Imposition of a long-overdue arms embargo by the UN Security Council would be a tangible signal of international resolve, would be essential to prevent further squandering of the country's remaining resources, and would minimize the threat posed by spoilers—such as Kiir's and Machar's core partisans and family members—to the UN and AU administration. Given South Sudan's rudimentary road and airport infrastructure and relatively few access points, a UN arms embargo could be easily monitored and would quickly lead to a significant reduction in the large-scale import of munitions, which South Sudan has no indigenous capacity to produce. An embargo would also ground the attack helicopters that have been used by Kiir's government against civilian targets, as they are flown by foreign mercenaries rather than South Sudanese.

Outreach to Earn South Sudanese Support for an International Transitional Administration and Defuse Spoilers

Even if Kiir and Machar were forced out of South Sudanese politics, other powerful individuals, including Kiir's and Machar's core partisans and family members, could still obstruct the transitional administration in pursuit of personal ambitions. These forces could be isolated by leveraging the United States' unique standing as the most instrumental and consistent supporter of South Sudan's independence.

Influential SPLA generals and senior officers are loath to watch South Sudan descend into chaos because of the machinations of a political elite, and U.S.-led outreach to these individuals could persuade them to support the UN and AU administration. Having led the decades-long struggle for South Sudan's independence, these officers are gravely concerned about the growth of tribal militias whose allegiances are transient and whose proliferation has accelerated the breakdown of the state. Some influential senior security officials would also view an international transitional administration as preferable to the unilateral military intervention of one or more neighboring states—interventions that would be perceived by the South Sudanese as predatory even if the actions of those states were provoked by their legitimate security concerns. Important tribal leaders could also be persuaded of the relevant benefits of an international transitional administration that would constrain and channel involvement of states in the region into a third-party peace intervention force.

Given the tribal cleavages that the past three years of violence have created and which the twenty-eight-states decree has exacerbated, those who have lost out in the reorganization—deposed from positions of power, denied access to resources or land, excluded from elite representation in Juba, and so on—could also be persuaded through U.S. diplomatic outreach to support an international transitional administration that repealed this decree and allowed for a more legitimate process in which the South Sudanese body politic—rather than Kiir, his regime, and the hard-line Dinka politicians of the Jieng Council of Elders—determined the structure and boundaries of the states.

Sustained High-Level Diplomacy to Secure Regional Support for an International Transitional Administration

The United States should work with states in the region and the AU to design an international transitional administration as the only viable mechanism to protect their interests after the collapse of the August 2015 agreement, in accordance with the AU principle of non-indifference that arose after the Rwandan genocide. The support of Uganda, Ethiopia, Sudan, and Kenya for this transition would minimize opposition from other African states amid inevitable allegations of neocolonialism. This would culminate in a call by IGAD and the AU to the UN Security Council for a resolution to establish the architecture for the transition, consistent with a request by South Sudan.

For Uganda, a credible security architecture—including but not limited to a third-party force—that ensures a buffer against Sudanese influence in South Sudan, the prevention of which is a core Ugandan strategic interest, would be critical. The tentative rapprochement between Sudan and Uganda that began following Ugandan President Yoweri Museveni's 2015 visit to Khartoum could provide a basis for a mutually beneficial understanding on the future political dispensation for South Sudan. The international transitional administration in South Sudan would also moderate the increasing competition between Uganda and Ethiopia for regional hegemony. Finally, a modicum of stability during a transitional UN and AU administration would revive opportunities for Ugandan commercial activity.

A role in the political and security structure of the international transitional administration would provide Ethiopia, which invested significant political capital in negotiating the August 2015 agreement, an opportunity to preserve its prestige and credibility. An effective transitional administration would also stem the flow of South Sudanese refugees into Ethiopia, which increased from just under fifty-five thousand before December 2013 to nearly two hundred twenty-five thousand by July 2016, and ultimately facilitate their return home, lessening ethnic conflict in eastern Ethiopia caused by the refugees' presence at a time of increasing ethnic unrest in other parts of the country.[49] The international transitional administration would also preempt a unilateral Ethiopian military intervention in South Sudan undertaken in the interests of regional stability or to counter other states' ambitions.

Sudan's concurrence with an international transitional administration would be based on two factors. The first is the expectation of increased and more regular oil production as a result of an end to the war and revenue transfers to Khartoum on the favorable basis of the current oil-sharing agreement, which is scheduled for renegotiation and on which South Sudan is already defaulting. The second is the curbing of support from South Sudan for Sudanese rebel groups.

The August 2015 agreement required all nonstate armed groups operating in South Sudan, such as the SPLM-North and the Darfuri Justice and Equality Movement, to withdraw from the country before the TGoNU was established, but this did not happen. While Sudan has actively negotiated with Kiir over these armed groups as well as on oil-sharing and the disputed territory of Abyei, Khartoum doubts that Kiir can or will abide by commitments he might make on these issues. An international administration would therefore provide more reliable assurances that Sudan's security and economic concerns will be addressed over the long term. Although the governance, human rights, and humanitarian crises from which the Sudanese rebel movements arose would need to be resolved separately, an international transitional administration in South Sudan might provide a new impetus for breaking the current stalemate in that political process.

Kenya played a leading role in negotiating the Comprehensive Peace Agreement that yielded South Sudan's independence in 2011. Moreover, President Uhuru Kenyatta personally negotiated the release of the Group of Ten (G10) political leaders following their detention in December 2013 and has been involved in other major diplomatic initiatives since the outbreak of the civil war. A UN and AU administration would serve Kenyan interests by stabilizing the long-standing commercial ties between South Sudan and Kenya, where much South Sudanese wealth is held, and by mitigating the possible exploitation of a security vacuum by extremist groups in South Sudan.

Diplomatic Campaign with Security Council Members and Donor Countries to Secure Endorsement and Financing of an International Transitional Administration

For the United Kingdom and France, the cost of supporting the proposed transition framework would be comparable to—and is more likely to give a positive return on investment than—the combined costs of their assessed dues to the current UNMISS operating budget and the ongoing bilateral and EU foreign assistance contributions to South Sudan, in the face of a worsening situation. Importantly, South Sudan's oil revenues, handled in a transparent and accountable manner, could partially fund service delivery. For China, the assurance of increased and sustained oil production facilitated by greater stability in South Sudan would be appealing; it would be incumbent on China to help to prevent a Russian veto to a UN Security Council endorsement of the transitional administration. This would necessarily follow a request to the Security Council from South Sudan, IGAD, the AU, and South Sudan's neighbors for the transitional administration, thereby discouraging Russian obstruction, as it rarely opposes unified African positions on matters that do not directly affect its interests.

Finally, donors and international financial institutions such as the World Bank and the IMF could be reassured by the accountability and transparency mechanisms governing the delivery of nonhumanitarian assistance under the transitional administration; this would bolster donor confidence that resources are supporting national strategies to meet the needs of South Sudanese citizens and unblock generous aid packages that provide additional incentives to South Sudanese constituencies to support the transition.

Conclusion

Despite the United States' multibillion-dollar annual commitment to South Sudan and intensive diplomatic effort to support its transition to independence, the country is facing a security and humanitarian catastrophe of epic scale that threatens not only its citizens but also the stability of a region in which the United States has invested heavily. The status quo is unsustainable for South Sudan, for neighboring states, and for donors attempting to arrest the grave human suffering but who are increasingly unable to do so in the hostile political environment that the war's protagonists have created. A new U.S. policy should be based on safeguarding South Sudan's sovereignty while empowering its people to build a state grounded in a legitimate and enduring social contract. An international transitional administration with an executive mandate is the most realistic path if such an endogenous South Sudanese effort is to succeed.

Appendix: Precedents for an International Transitional Administration

The authorities and administrative mechanisms contemplated under an international transitional administration in South Sudan are not without precedent. Each of the cases below differs from the other and from South Sudan in myriad ways, including the political environment, the size of the territory in question, the degree to which the designated mandates and authorities were exercised, the credibility of the transitional institutions among the local population, and the level of opposition to their establishment. As is inevitable in fragile states and conflict-affected environments, these cases also entailed many implementation challenges, including lengthy deployment timelines for peacekeepers and civilian staff. Nevertheless, these examples provide constructive lessons. [50]

BOSNIA AND HERZEGOVINA

The 1995 Dayton Peace Agreement designated a high representative to oversee implementation of the civilian aspects of the accord. A Peace Implementation Council (PIC) of fifty-five countries and international organizations was established shortly after the agreement was signed to support implementation, and the Steering Board was created as a subset of the PIC to provide political guidance to the high representative. While the high representative's initial mandate focused on monitoring implementation and coordinating the work of the civilian institutions and agencies in Bosnia and Herzegovina, at a December 1997 meeting in Bonn, Germany, the PIC conferred on the high representative the power to remove officials who violated the agreement and to impose the necessary laws if legislative bodies failed to do so. [51] These subsequently became known as the Bonn powers.

KOSOVO

Following the withdrawal of Serbian forces from Kosovo, the 1999 UN Security Council resolution that established the international security presence also authorized the UN Secretary-General to establish an international civil presence in Kosovo to provide an interim administration. At the time, the United Nations determined that public service structures were "largely inoperative due to a combination of neglect, war damage, and the departure of trained staff."[52] A special representative with executive authority, including the right to appoint and remove personnel for civil administrative and judicial functions and the authority to administer funds and property of the former Yugoslavia and the Republic of Serbia in the territory of Kosovo, was appointed to head the UN Interim Administration Mission in Kosovo (UNMIK).

The civil administration was charged with establishing multiethnic governing structures to deliver public services for as long as required before transferring them to self-governing institutions established under a political settlement.[53] These powers included oversight of the judiciary and civilian police. A deputy special representative was mandated to oversee three functional departments covering areas where rudimentary or no legitimate local structures existed (police, judicial affairs, and economic affairs and natural resources administration); three secretariats where some local structures were in place (education, social welfare and labor, and health); and a municipal support services unit. The Department of Economic and Natural Resources supervised industry, trade and commerce, public utilities, post and telecommunications, transport, agricultural and rural development, and environmental protection. Five regional administrators were also designated. More than 1,200 international civilian staff oversaw service administration. UNMIK's initial annual budget was $650 million, of which nearly $380 million (in 2016 dollars) was allocated for the civilian staff component of the interim administration. UNMIK was funded through assessed contributions to the UN.

CAMBODIA

Following the signing of the Agreements on a Comprehensive Political Settlement of the Cambodia Conflict in Paris in 1991, the UN Security Council established the UN Transitional Authority in Cambodia

(UNTAC), to which the Supreme National Council (SNC) of Cambodia, composed of the four Cambodian factions, delegated "all powers necessary" to ensure the implementation of those peace agreements.[54] The SNC was "the unique legitimate body and source of authority in which, throughout the transitional period, the sovereignty, independence and unity of Cambodia [were] enshrined" and was charged with providing guidance to UNTAC.[55] The Special Representative of the Secretary-General (SRSG) was empowered to override domestic decisions that did not conform to the peace agreements (although the special representative never exercised this power). In addition, if no consensus was reached within the SNC and the chairman of the SNC was unable to provide guidance to UNTAC, decision-making powers transferred to the SRSG.

The Paris Agreements defined the end of the transitional period as when an elected constituent assembly approved a new constitution and transformed itself into a legislative assembly. Given the consequent importance of elections, those institutions deemed as directly influencing the outcome of elections were placed under direct UN supervision as part of an Interim Joint Administration; these included foreign affairs, national defense, finance, and public security and information. The SRSG was mandated to issue directives to the relevant agencies and offices, to remove or reassign staff, and to place UN personnel in staff positions. UNTAC also supervised the police and, in consultation with the SNC, other law enforcement and judicial processes. Twenty-one provisional offices were established to parallel local administrative structures.

In addition to a peacekeeping force of fifteen thousand, a civilian police force of three thousand, and more than a thousand international electoral supervisors, three hundred international staff were deployed to execute UNTAC's civil administration mandate. UNTAC's total expenditures for the first eighteen months of the mission were approximately $1.9 billion (in 2016 dollars).[56] UNTAC was funded through assessed contributions to the UN.

EAST TIMOR

The UN Transitional Administration in East Timor (UNTAET) was established in 1999 after the UN Mission in East Timor collapsed in the wake of mass violence. UNTAET consisted of a governance and public administration component involving nearly one thousand international staff, a civilian police force of two thousand, and an armed UN peace-keeping force of more than nine thousand. UNTAET was fully respon-sible for the administration of the country until 2002, with a mandate to provide security and maintain law and order, establish an effective administration, assist in social service development, ensure the coor-dination and delivery of humanitarian and development assistance, support capacity-building for self-government, and assist in the estab-lishment of conditions for sustainable development.

UNTAET's first SRSG, in consultation with East Timorese political leadership, established the National Consultative Council, consisting of eleven East Timorese and four UNTAET officials to oversee the deci-sion-making process during the transitional period. The deputy SRSG for governance and public administration oversaw the work of five administrative divisions: judicial affairs; civilian police; economic, finan-cial, and development affairs; public services; and electoral operations. The total annual expenditure for UNTAET once the civil administration was fully in place was approximately $700 million (in 2016 dollars), paid for through assessed contributions to the United Nations.[57]

LIBERIA

In 2005, a European Commission audit documented extensive evidence of widespread corruption in the National Transitional Government of Liberia (NTGL), established in 2003 as part of a peace agreement and after Charles Taylor's exit from power. Donors subsequently used their funding leverage—including the threat of an embargo on foreign assistance—to forge an agreement with the NTGL on an oversight and accountability mechanism to include international experts in Liberian institutions to manage revenue, monitor and supervise budgets, and handle procurement. These experts had cosignatory authority on all financial transactions. The AU and the Economic Community of West Africa States managed discussions with the NTGL to reach the agree-ment to establish the Governance and Economic Management Assis-tance Program (GEMAP).

GEMAP initially involved the Ministry of Finance; the Bureau of Budget; the Ministry of Lands, Mines, and Energy; the General Services

Administration; and four state-owned companies—the National Port Authority, the Roberts International Airport, the Liberia Petroleum Refining Company, and the Forestry Development Authority. The Ministry of Public Works, the Ministry of Planning and Economic Affairs, and the Monrovia City Corporation were subsequently incorporated into the mechanism. An Economic Governance Steering Committee—co-chaired by the president of Liberia and the U.S. ambassador to Liberia with the participation of other donors and international institutions, including the United Nations and the World Bank—oversaw GEMAP.

Endnotes

1. Author's calculation of all State Department and U.S. Agency for International Development assistance to South Sudan from fiscal year 2005–2006 through 2015–2016.
2. Øystein H. Rolandsen, "Small and Far Between: Peacekeeping Economies in South Sudan," Journal of Intervention and Statebuilding 9, no. 3 (2015): 355–56.
3. On June 1, 2016, former Botswanan President Festus Mogae, chairperson of the Joint Monitoring and Evaluation Commission, reported that the level of violence in South Sudan had not diminished despite the formation of the transitional unity government. See Daniel Finnan, "Violence Continues in South Sudan Despite New Unity Government," Radio France Internationale, June 1, 2016, http://allafrica.com/stories/201606020089.html. In his report of June 30, 2016, General Molla Hailemariam, chairman of the Ceasefire and Transitional Security Arrangements Monitoring Mechanism, stated, "Recent weeks have witnessed limited progress in the implementation of the [permanent ceasefire and transitional security arrangements]. It is worrisome that violence continued to occur, as evidenced by the clashes that broke out in Kajo-Keji, Central Equatoria, Raja, Western Bahr El Ghazal, Leer, Unity State and the most recent and appalling fighting in Wau, Western Bahr El Ghazal last week." See Radio Tamazuj, "Full Statement of General Molla Hailemariam, Chairman of CTSAMM," June 30, 2016, http://radiotamazuj.org/en/article/full-statement-general-molla-hailemariam-chairman-ctsamm.
4. Kenneth Pollack and Barbara F. Walter, "Escaping the Civil War Trap in the Middle East," Washington Quarterly 38, no. 2 (Summer 2015): 34; see also I. William Zartman, Ripe for Resolution: Conflict and Intervention in Africa (New York: Oxford University Press, 1989).
5. "Framework for Analysis for Atrocity Crimes: A Tool for Prevention," United Nations, 2014.
6. "Final Report of the African Union Commission of Inquiry on South Sudan," October 15, 2014, http://peaceau.org/uploads/auciss.final.report.pdf, p. 225.
7. John Young, "Popular Struggles and Elite Co-optation: The Nuer White Army in South Sudan's Civil War," HSBA Working Paper 41, Small Arms Survey, Graduate Institute of International Development Studies, Geneva, Switzerland, July 2016, pp. 15–17.
8. "Final Report of the African Union Commission of Inquiry on South Sudan," pp. 223–29.
9. Hundreds of soldiers aligned with Salva Kiir and Riek Machar were killed in a firefight in Juba on July 8, 2016.
10. The 1993 Arusha Accords signed between the Rwandan government and the Rwandan Patriotic Front (RPF) provided for deployment of one RPF battalion to Kigali. This battalion entered Kigali in January 1994, four months before the onset of the genocide. That January, the U.S. Mission to the United Nations cabled the U.S. Embassy in Kigali

with a report of a meeting with the UN Department of Peacekeeping Operations' Hedi Annabi, warning that "the combination of increasing covert activities and a stalemated political process could produce a potentially explosive atmosphere.... The government is actively involved in distributing arms and training its militia; these covert activities are particularly disturbing given the presence of an RPF battalion in Kigali." In Rwanda, the UN peacekeeping mission was providing protection to the RPF battalion and important individuals as well as to the residences of the president and prime minister, which is not even the case in South Sudan. Numerous differences between Rwanda in 1994 and South Sudan in 2016 aside, history provides a cautionary lesson.

11. "Report from the Chairperson of the Joint Monitoring and Evaluation Commission (JMEC) for the Agreement on the Resolution of the Conflict in the Republic of South Sudan to the African Union Peace and Security Council (PSC)," January 29, 2016, p. 3, http://jmecsouthsudan.org/uploads/AUPSCreport.pdf. In June 2016, Kiir and Machar agreed to a national commission with representatives of all parties, the Troika, and South Africa and Tanzania to determine the number of states in South Sudan. However, this commission has not begun its work yet.

12. See "Note to correspondents on the Special Investigation and UNHQ Board of Inquiry into the violence in the UNMISS Protection of Civilians site in February 2016," https://www.un.org/sg/en/content/sg/note-correspondents/2016-06-21/note-correspondents-special-investigation-and-unhq-board. See also http://www.reuters.com/article/us-southsudan-unrest-un-idUSKCN0Z731G

13. Chester A. Crocker, "The Diplomacy of Engagement in Transitional Polities," in Chester A. Crocker, Fen Osler Hampson, and Pamela Aall, eds., *Managing Conflict in a World Adrift* (Washington, DC: U.S. Institute of Peace, 2015), p. 398.

14. David A. Lake, "Practical Sovereignty and Postconflict Governance," in Chester A. Crocker, Fen Osler Hampson, and Pamela Aall, eds., *Managing Conflict in a World Adrift* (Washington, DC: U.S. Institute of Peace, 2015), pp. 301–2.

15. The Jieng Council of Elders has repeatedly developed hard-line policy proposals, subsequently adopted by Kiir, including drafting the reservations to the peace agreement that Kiir issued upon reluctantly signing it in August 2015 and the initial draft of the decree to expand South Sudan from ten to twenty-eight states. More recently, the Jieng Council was instrumental in publicly opposing the call from IGAD and the UN Security Council for an international protection force.

16. "Practical Sovereignty and Postconflict Governance," p. 305.

17. Festus Mogae, "Opening Statement of the JMEC Chair at the Plenary of 23 June 2016," transcript, June 23, 2016, http://jmecsouthsudan.org/news.php?id=31.

18. Statement by Festus Mogae, Chairperson of JMEC, to the JMEC Partner's Meeting on the Status of the Implementation of the Agreement on the Resolution of the Conflict in the Republic of South Sudan, July 31, 2016, Khartoum, Sudan.

19. "Opening Statement of the JMEC Chair."

20. "Final Report of the African Union Commission of Inquiry on South Sudan," pp. 106, 276.

21. As political scientist Samuel Huntington observed several decades ago, power operates in two dimensions: it can be expanded and contracted as well as concentrated and dispersed. In contrast to the conventional wisdom in the United States that "power is something which may be lying around on the floor of the capitol or the presidential palace and that a group of conspirators may sneak in and run off with," Huntington recognized that many countries in conflict face not a zero-sum contestation for power but an absence of power. In such states, he argued, the challenge is "to make power, to mobilize groups into politics, and to organize their participation in politics." See Samuel P. Huntington, *Political Order in Changing Societies* (New Haven, CT: Yale

University Press, 1968), pp. 143–45.

22. UN Security Council resolution 2241 requested the Secretary-General to conduct an assessment of the "security planning in Juba" and "the appropriate role for the United Nations in providing security to key infrastructure." The UN Department of Peacekeeping provided this assessment to the Security Council in December 2015 and argued that security in Juba could only be ensured politically, not by UNMISS intervention. Indeed, during the outbreak of limited fighting between SPLA and SPLA-IO forces in Juba on July 8, 2016, UNMISS did not conduct any patrols.

23. "Communique of the Second IGAD Plus Extraordinary Summit on the Situation in the Republic of South Sudan," August 5, 2016, Addis Ababa, Ethiopia and UN Security Council resolution 2304.

24. "Final Report of the African Union Commission of Inquiry on South Sudan."

25. Peter Martell, "South Sudan Is Dying, and Nobody Is Counting," Agence France Press, March 10, 2016. See also Nicholas Kristof, "South Sudan: Where the Soldiers Are Scarier Than the Crocodiles," New York Times, March 12, 2016. See also Syrian Observatory for Human Rights, "More than 370000 People Are Thought to Be Killed Since the Rise of Syrian Revolution," last modified February 2, 2016, http://syriahr.com/en/?p=44437.

26. Office of the Deputy Humanitarian Coordinator for South Sudan, "Crisis Impacts on Households in Unity State, South Sudan, 2014–2015: Initial Results of a Survey," January 2016, pp. 21–23, http://reliefweb.int/report/south-sudan/crisis-impacts-households-unity-state-south-sudan-2014-2015-initial-results.

27. The estimate is from violence in Guit, Koch, Leer, Mayendit, and Panyijar counties in Unity State, South Sudan, over approximately twelve months starting the fourth quarter of 2014. According to a statement issued on March 18, 2016, the Office of the UN High Commissioner for Human Rights recorded 3,218 civilians killed in Yemen from March 25, 2015, to March 17, 2016 .

28. Aide-Memoire, "International Monetary Fund 2016 Article IV Consultation with the Government of the Republic of South Sudan," May 31, 2016. See also Festus Mogae, "Opening Statement of the JMEC Chair at the Plenary of 23 June 2016."

29. International Monetary Fund, "IMF Staff Completes 2016 Article IV Mission to South Sudan," news release, June 1, 2016, http://imf.org/external/np/sec/pr/2016/pr16259.htm.

30. Famine Early Warning Systems Network, "Food Security Outlook Update: Staple Food Prices Increasing More Rapidly Than Expected," April 2016, http://fews.net/east-africa/south-sudan/food-security-outlook-update/april-2016.

31. These 2015 designations were the first time that the UN Office for the Coordination of Humanitarian Affairs (OCHA) identified four simultaneous level 3 emergencies: South Sudan, Iraq, Yemen, and Syria. The Inter-Agency Standing Committee of international humanitarian actors defines level 3 emergencies as "major sudden-onset humanitarian crises triggered by natural disasters or conflict which require system-wide mobilization." Five criteria are used to determine whether a level 3 response is required: scale, urgency, complexity, combined national and international capacity to respond, and reputational risk. See Inter-Agency Standing Committee, "Humanitarian System-Wide Emergency Activation: Definition and Procedures," April 13, 2012, http://interagencystandingcommittee.org/system/files/legacy_files/2.%20System-Wide%20%28Level%203%29%20Activation%20%2820Apr12%29.pdf.

32. UN High Commissioner for Refugees, "Refugees Fleeing South Sudan Pass One Million Mark," September 16, 2016, http://unhcr.org/en-us/news/latest/2016/9/57dbe2d94/refugees-fleeing-south-sudan-pass-million-mark.html.

33. OCHA, Humanitarian Bulletin: South Sudan no. 14, September 22, 2016, http://

reliefweb.int/sites/reliefweb.int/files/resources/OCHA_SouthSudan_humanitarian
_bulletin_12.pdf; see also Food and Agriculture Organization, World Food Program,
and UNICEF, "Unprecedented Level of Food Insecurity in South Sudan," news
release, June 29, 2016, http://unicef.org/media/media_91776.html.

34. The Uganda People's Defense Force (UPDF) was deployed to South Sudan in the
early days of the war and was instrumental in preventing an opposition attack on
Juba in January 2014 and in reclaiming Bor in Jonglei State for the government
shortly thereafter. The UPDF withdrew in October 2015 as part of the August 2015
agreement. The Ethiopian military has undertaken contingency planning for a
military intervention and already has two battalions in South Sudan as part of the UN
Mission in South Sudan. Ethiopian Prime Minister Hailemariam Desalegn privately
threatened Ugandan President Yoweri Museveni with unilateral military intervention
to force the UPDF out of South Sudan in 2015. Even if that threat was a tactical move to
induce Museveni to pressure Kiir to accept the IGAD agreement, such rhetoric risks
spiraling into action under certain circumstances.

35. At the end of January 2016, fighting broke out between Nuer and Anuak communities
in Gambella, Ethiopia. In April, Murle militia from South Sudan launched an attack in
Gambella against Nuer communities, which precipitated an Ethiopian counterattack
across the border. As of June 2016, Ethiopian troops were still deployed inside South
Sudan. These developments directly result from population displacement out of South
Sudan and compound ethnic tensions within Ethiopia.

36. Nicholas Haysom and Sean Kane, "Understanding the Transition: A Challenge
and Opportunity for Mediators," Center for International Cooperation, New York
University, June 2013, pp. 3–4.

37. David A. Lake and Christopher J. Fariss, "Why International Trusteeship Fails:
The Politics of External Authority in Areas of Limited Statehood," *Governance: An
International Journal of Policy, Administration, and Institutions* 27, no. 1 (2014): 6, 11, 17.

38. For other cases that can provide constructive lessons for an international transitional
administration in South Sudan, see the appendix.

39. Princeton Lyman, Jon Temin, and Susan Stigant, "Crisis and Opportunity in South
Sudan," United States Institute of Peace, Peace Brief 164, 2014, p. 4, http://www.usip.
org/publications/crisis-and-opportunity-in-south-sudan.

40. In 2014 and 2015, the South Sudan Law Society conducted a survey among a
representative sample of South Sudanese across ethnic groups, socioeconomic
statuses, livelihood strategies, geographic location, and exposure to conflict using the
Harvard trauma questionnaire and concluded that 41 percent exhibited symptoms of
post-traumatic stress disorder, rates comparable to those in post-genocide Rwanda
and post-genocide Cambodia.

41. "Final Report of the African Union Commission of Inquiry on South Sudan," pp.
282–83.

42. Ibid, p. 275.

43. Ibid, pp. 279, 303.

44. See "Note to correspondents on the Special Investigation and UNHQ Board of Inquiry
into the violence in the UNMISS Protection of Civilians site in February 2016," June 21,
2016: http://www.un.org/sg/offthecuff/index.asp?nid=4585. See also "MSF internal
review of the February 2016 attack on the Malakal Protection of Civilians Site and the
post-event situation," Medecins Sans Frontiers, June 2016: http://www.msf.org/sites/
msf.org/files/malakal_report_210616_pc.pdf.

45. Bruce Jones, "The UN Security Council and Crisis Management: Still Central After
All of These Years," in *Managing Conflict in a World Adrift*, p. 319.

46. "Final Report of the African Union Commission of Inquiry on South Sudan," p. 299.

47. Festus Mogae, "Statement by the JMEC Chairperson to the AU Peace and Security Council," January 29, 2016, http://www.jmecsouthsudan.com/news.php?id=11.

48. For a detailed explanation and analysis of preemptive contract sanctions, see "Preventing Odious Obligations: A New Tool for Protecting Citizens from Illegitimate Regimes," Center for Global Development, 2010, http://faculty.wcas.northwestern.edu/~sjv340/cgd_report.pdf.

49. UN High Commissioner for Refugees, "South Sudan Situation: Information Sharing Portal," http://data.unhcr.org/SouthSudan/country.php?id=65.

50. The author would like to thank the United States Institute of Peace for research on previous instances of international governing arrangements.

51. See "Mandate," on the Office of the High Representative's official website, http://www.ohr.int/?page_id=1161.

52. "Report of the Secretary-General on the United Nations Interim Administration Mission in Kosovo," July 12, 1999, http://www.un.org/en/ga/search/view_doc.asp?symbol=S/1999/779.

53. Ibid. The civil administration in Kosovo was separate from the institution-building component authorized by the UN Security Council, which was led by the Organization for Security and Co-operation in Europe.

54. "United Nations Transitional Administration in Cambodia: Establishment of UNTAC," http://www.un.org/en/peacekeeping/missions/past/untacbackgr2.html.

55. United Nations Department of Public Information, "Agreements on a Comprehensive Political Settlement of the Cambodia Conflict," October 23, 1991, http://usip.org/sites/default/files/file/resources/collections/peace_agreements/agree_comppol_10231991.pdf.

56. UN General Assembly, 47th Session, "Agenda Item 123: Financing of the UN Transitional Authority in Cambodia; Report of the Secretary-General; Addendum" July 27, 1993, http://www.un.org/ga/search/view_doc.asp?symbol=A/47/733/ADD.1.

57. United Nations, "Report of Secretary-General on the United Nations Transitional Administration in East Timor," S/2002/432, April 17, 2002, http://documents-dds-ny.un.org/doc/UNDOC/GEN/N02/327/74/IMG/N0232774.pdf.

About the Author

Kate Almquist Knopf is director of the Africa Center for Strategic Studies, an academic institution within the U.S. Department of Defense based at the National Defense University in Washington, DC. Almquist Knopf has spent most of her career focused on the intersection of security and development in Africa. From 2001 to 2009, she held several senior positions at the U.S. Agency for International Development, including as assistant administrator for Africa, Sudan mission director, deputy assistant administrator for Africa, and special assistant and senior policy advisor to the administrator. Almquist Knopf has also been senior advisor for the Crisis Management Initiative, a conflict mediation organization founded by former Finnish President and Nobel Laureate Martti Ahtisaari, and a visiting policy fellow at the Center for Global Development. Prior to federal service, she was chief of staff for the Massachusetts Turnpike Authority and for the Executive Office for Administration and Finance of the Commonwealth of Massachusetts. She began her career at World Vision, an international nongovernmental organization. Almquist Knopf holds a BA in international relations from Johns Hopkins University and an MA in international relations with concentrations in African studies and conflict management from the university's School of Advanced International Studies.

Advisory Committee for
Ending South Sudan's Civil War

David S. Abramowitz
Humanity United

Reuben E. Brigety II
George Washington University

Elizabeth M. Cousens
United Nations Foundation

Chester A. Crocker
Georgetown University

Alan Goulty
*Woodrow Wilson International Center for
Scholars*

Cameron R. Hume
Independent Consultant

Nancy E. Lindborg
United States Institute of Peace

Princeton N. Lyman
United States Institute of Peace

Michael Moran
Control Risks Group

Andrew S. Natsios
Texas A&M University

Stewart M. Patrick, *ex officio*
Council on Foreign Relations

John P. Prendergast
Enough Project

David H. Shinn
George Washington University

Paul B. Stares, *ex officio*
Council on Foreign Relations

Paul D. Williams
George Washington University

William Zartman
*Johns Hopkins School of Advanced
International Studies*

Mission Statement of the
Center for Preventive Action

The Center for Preventive Action (CPA) seeks to help prevent, defuse, or resolve deadly conflicts around the world and to expand the body of knowledge on conflict prevention. It does so by creating a forum in which representatives of governments, international organizations, nongovernmental organizations, corporations, and civil society can gather to develop operational and timely strategies for promoting peace in specific conflict situations. The center focuses on conflicts in countries or regions that affect U.S. interests but may be otherwise overlooked, where prevention appears possible and when the resources of the Council on Foreign Relations can make a difference. The center does this by

- issuing Council Special Reports to evaluate and respond rapidly to developing conflict situations and formulate timely, concrete policy recommendations that the U.S. government and international and local actors can use to limit the potential for deadly violence;

- engaging the U.S. government and news media in conflict prevention efforts by briefing administration officials and members of Congress on CPA findings and recommendations, facilitating contacts between U.S. officials and important local and external actors, and raising awareness among journalists of potential flashpoints around the globe;

- building networks with international organizations and institutions to complement and leverage the Council's established influence in the U.S. policy arena and increase the impact of CPA recommendations; and

- providing a source of expertise on conflict prevention to include research, case studies, and lessons learned from past conflicts that policymakers and private citizens can use to prevent or mitigate future deadly conflicts.

Council Special Reports

Published by the Council on Foreign Relations

Repairing the U.S.-Israel Relationship
Robert D. Blackwill and Philip H. Gordon; CSR No. 76, November 2016

Securing a Democratic Future for Myanmar
Priscilla A. Clapp; CSR No. 75, March 2016
A Center for Preventive Action Report

Xi Jinping on the Global Stage: Chinese Foreign Policy Under a Powerful but Exposed Leader
Robert D. Blackwill and Kurt M. Campbell; CSR No. 74, February 2016
An International Institutions and Global Governance Program Report

Enhancing U.S. Support for Peace Operations in Africa
Paul D. Williams; CSR No. 73, May 2015

Revising U.S. Grand Strategy Toward China
Robert D. Blackwill and Ashley J. Tellis; CSR No. 72, March 2015
An International Institutions and Global Governance Program Report

Strategic Stability in the Second Nuclear Age
Gregory D. Koblentz; CSR No. 71, November 2014

U.S. Policy to Counter Nigeria's Boko Haram
John Campbell; CSR No. 70, November 2014
A Center for Preventive Action Report

Limiting Armed Drone Proliferation
Micah Zenko and Sarah Kreps; CSR No. 69, June 2014
A Center for Preventive Action Report

Reorienting U.S. Pakistan Strategy: From Af-Pak to Asia
Daniel S. Markey; CSR No. 68, January 2014

Afghanistan After the Drawdown
Seth G. Jones and Keith Crane; CSR No. 67, November 2013
A Center for Preventive Action Report

The Future of U.S. Special Operations Forces
Linda Robinson; CSR No. 66, April 2013

Reforming U.S. Drone Strike Policies
Micah Zenko; CSR No. 65, January 2013
A Center for Preventive Action Report

Countering Criminal Violence in Central America
Michael Shifter; CSR No. 64, April 2012
A Center for Preventive Action Report

Saudi Arabia in the New Middle East
F. Gregory Gause III; CSR No. 63, December 2011
A Center for Preventive Action Report

Partners in Preventive Action: The United States and International Institutions
Paul B. Stares and Micah Zenko; CSR No. 62, September 2011
A Center for Preventive Action Report

Justice Beyond The Hague: Supporting the Prosecution of International Crimes in National Courts
David A. Kaye; CSR No. 61, June 2011

The Drug War in Mexico: Confronting a Shared Threat
David A. Shirk; CSR No. 60, March 2011
A Center for Preventive Action Report

UN Security Council Enlargement and U.S. Interests
Kara C. McDonald and Stewart M. Patrick; CSR No. 59, December 2010
An International Institutions and Global Governance Program Report

Congress and National Security
Kay King; CSR No. 58, November 2010

Toward Deeper Reductions in U.S. and Russian Nuclear Weapons
Micah Zenko; CSR No. 57, November 2010
A Center for Preventive Action Report

Internet Governance in an Age of Cyber Insecurity
Robert K. Knake; CSR No. 56, September 2010
An International Institutions and Global Governance Program Report

From Rome to Kampala: The U.S. Approach to the 2010 International Criminal Court Review Conference
Vijay Padmanabhan; CSR No. 55, April 2010

Strengthening the Nuclear Nonproliferation Regime
Paul Lettow; CSR No. 54, April 2010
An International Institutions and Global Governance Program Report

The Russian Economic Crisis
Jeffrey Mankoff; CSR No. 53, April 2010

Somalia: A New Approach
Bronwyn E. Bruton; CSR No. 52, March 2010
A Center for Preventive Action Report

The Future of NATO
James M. Goldgeier; CSR No. 51, February 2010
An International Institutions and Global Governance Program Report

The United States in the New Asia
Evan A. Feigenbaum and Robert A. Manning; CSR No. 50, November 2009
An International Institutions and Global Governance Program Report

Intervention to Stop Genocide and Mass Atrocities: International Norms and U.S. Policy
Matthew C. Waxman; CSR No. 49, October 2009
An International Institutions and Global Governance Program Report

Enhancing U.S. Preventive Action
Paul B. Stares and Micah Zenko; CSR No. 48, October 2009
A Center for Preventive Action Report

The Canadian Oil Sands: Energy Security vs. Climate Change
Michael A. Levi; CSR No. 47, May 2009
A Maurice R. Greenberg Center for Geoeconomic Studies Report

The National Interest and the Law of the Sea
Scott G. Borgerson; CSR No. 46, May 2009

Lessons of the Financial Crisis
Benn Steil; CSR No. 45, March 2009
A Maurice R. Greenberg Center for Geoeconomic Studies Report

Global Imbalances and the Financial Crisis
Steven Dunaway; CSR No. 44, March 2009
A Maurice R. Greenberg Center for Geoeconomic Studies Report

Eurasian Energy Security
Jeffrey Mankoff; CSR No. 43, February 2009

Preparing for Sudden Change in North Korea
Paul B. Stares and Joel S. Wit; CSR No. 42, January 2009
A Center for Preventive Action Report

Averting Crisis in Ukraine
Steven Pifer; CSR No. 41, January 2009
A Center for Preventive Action Report

Congo: Securing Peace, Sustaining Progress
Anthony W. Gambino; CSR No. 40, October 2008
A Center for Preventive Action Report

Deterring State Sponsorship of Nuclear Terrorism
Michael A. Levi; CSR No. 39, September 2008

China, Space Weapons, and U.S. Security
Bruce W. MacDonald; CSR No. 38, September 2008

Sovereign Wealth and Sovereign Power: The Strategic Consequences of American Indebtedness
Brad W. Setser; CSR No. 37, September 2008
A Maurice R. Greenberg Center for Geoeconomic Studies Report

Securing Pakistan's Tribal Belt
Daniel S. Markey; CSR No. 36, July 2008 (web-only release) and August 2008
A Center for Preventive Action Report

Avoiding Transfers to Torture
Ashley S. Deeks; CSR No. 35, June 2008

Global FDI Policy: Correcting a Protectionist Drift
David M. Marchick and Matthew J. Slaughter; CSR No. 34, June 2008
A Maurice R. Greenberg Center for Geoeconomic Studies Report

Dealing with Damascus: Seeking a Greater Return on U.S.-Syria Relations
Mona Yacoubian and Scott Lasensky; CSR No. 33, June 2008
A Center for Preventive Action Report

Climate Change and National Security: An Agenda for Action
Joshua W. Busby; CSR No. 32, November 2007
A Maurice R. Greenberg Center for Geoeconomic Studies Report

Planning for Post-Mugabe Zimbabwe
Michelle D. Gavin; CSR No. 31, October 2007
A Center for Preventive Action Report

The Case for Wage Insurance
Robert J. LaLonde; CSR No. 30, September 2007
A Maurice R. Greenberg Center for Geoeconomic Studies Report

Reform of the International Monetary Fund
Peter B. Kenen; CSR No. 29, May 2007
A Maurice R. Greenberg Center for Geoeconomic Studies Report

Nuclear Energy: Balancing Benefits and Risks
Charles D. Ferguson; CSR No. 28, April 2007

Nigeria: Elections and Continuing Challenges
Robert I. Rotberg; CSR No. 27, April 2007
A Center for Preventive Action Report

The Economic Logic of Illegal Immigration
Gordon H. Hanson; CSR No. 26, April 2007
A Maurice R. Greenberg Center for Geoeconomic Studies Report

The United States and the WTO Dispute Settlement System
Robert Z. Lawrence; CSR No. 25, March 2007
A Maurice R. Greenberg Center for Geoeconomic Studies Report

Bolivia on the Brink
Eduardo A. Gamarra; CSR No. 24, February 2007
A Center for Preventive Action Report

After the Surge: The Case for U.S. Military Disengagement From Iraq
Steven N. Simon; CSR No. 23, February 2007

Darfur and Beyond: What Is Needed to Prevent Mass Atrocities
Lee Feinstein; CSR No. 22, January 2007

Avoiding Conflict in the Horn of Africa: U.S. Policy Toward Ethiopia and Eritrea
Terrence Lyons; CSR No. 21, December 2006
A Center for Preventive Action Report

Living with Hugo: U.S. Policy Toward Hugo Chávez's Venezuela
Richard Lapper; CSR No. 20, November 2006
A Center for Preventive Action Report

Reforming U.S. Patent Policy: Getting the Incentives Right
Keith E. Maskus; CSR No. 19, November 2006
A Maurice R. Greenberg Center for Geoeconomic Studies Report

Foreign Investment and National Security: Getting the Balance Right
Alan P. Larson and David M. Marchick; CSR No. 18, July 2006
A Maurice R. Greenberg Center for Geoeconomic Studies Report

Challenges for a Postelection Mexico: Issues for U.S. Policy
Pamela K. Starr; CSR No. 17, June 2006 (web-only release) and November 2006

U.S.-India Nuclear Cooperation: A Strategy for Moving Forward
Michael A. Levi and Charles D. Ferguson; CSR No. 16, June 2006

Generating Momentum for a New Era in U.S.-Turkey Relations
Steven A. Cook and Elizabeth Sherwood-Randall; CSR No. 15, June 2006

Peace in Papua: Widening a Window of Opportunity
Blair A. King; CSR No. 14, March 2006
A Center for Preventive Action Report

Neglected Defense: Mobilizing the Private Sector to Support Homeland Security
Stephen E. Flynn and Daniel B. Prieto; CSR No. 13, March 2006

Afghanistan's Uncertain Transition From Turmoil to Normalcy
Barnett R. Rubin; CSR No. 12, March 2006
A Center for Preventive Action Report

Preventing Catastrophic Nuclear Terrorism
Charles D. Ferguson; CSR No. 11, March 2006

Getting Serious About the Twin Deficits
Menzie D. Chinn; CSR No. 10, September 2005
A Maurice R. Greenberg Center for Geoeconomic Studies Report

Both Sides of the Aisle: A Call for Bipartisan Foreign Policy
Nancy E. Roman; CSR No. 9, September 2005

Forgotten Intervention? What the United States Needs to Do in the Western Balkans
Amelia Branczik and William L. Nash; CSR No. 8, June 2005
A Center for Preventive Action Report

A New Beginning: Strategies for a More Fruitful Dialogue with the Muslim World
Craig Charney and Nicole Yakatan; CSR No. 7, May 2005

Power-Sharing in Iraq
David L. Phillips; CSR No. 6, April 2005
A Center for Preventive Action Report

Giving Meaning to "Never Again": Seeking an Effective Response to the Crisis in Darfur and Beyond
Cheryl O. Igiri and Princeton N. Lyman; CSR No. 5, September 2004

Freedom, Prosperity, and Security: The G8 Partnership with Africa: Sea Island 2004 and Beyond
J. Brian Atwood, Robert S. Browne, and Princeton N. Lyman; CSR No. 4, May 2004

Addressing the HIV/AIDS Pandemic: A U.S. Global AIDS Strategy for the Long Term
Daniel M. Fox and Princeton N. Lyman; CSR No. 3, May 2004
Cosponsored with the Milbank Memorial Fund

Challenges for a Post-Election Philippines
Catharin E. Dalpino; CSR No. 2, May 2004
A Center for Preventive Action Report

Stability, Security, and Sovereignty in the Republic of Georgia
David L. Phillips; CSR No. 1, January 2004
A Center for Preventive Action Report

Note: Council Special Reports are available for download from CFR's website, www.cfr.org.
For more information, email publications@cfr.org.

www.ingramcontent.com/pod-product-compliance
Lightning Source LLC
Chambersburg PA
CBHW070801050426
42452CB00012B/2438